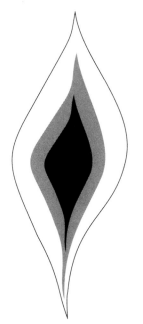

POWER FROM THE EARTH

Janet De Saulles

Wayland

Other titles in this series include:
Power from Plants
Power from the Sun
Power from Water
Power from the Wind

Cover: Using power from the Earth to make energy at a power station in New Zealand.

Designer: David Armitage

Picture acknowledgements
Energy Technology Support Unit 24, 25; Eye Ubiquitous 21; Geoscience Features 8, 13, 16, 19, 26; Hutchison Library 11, 14; Photri 27 (top); Science Photo Library 18; Survival Anglia 12, 17; Topham Picture Library 20, 27 (bottom); Zefa 4, 5, 15.

Text based on *Geothermal Energy* in the *Alternative Energy* series published in 1990.

First published in 1993 by
Wayland (Publishers) Limited
© Copyright Wayland (Publishers) Limited

British Library Cataloguing in Publication Data
De Saulles, Janet
Power from the Earth. - (Energy series)
I. Title II. Series
333.79
ISBN 0 7502 0813 9

Typeset by Perspective Marketing Limited

Printed in Italy by G. Canale & C.S.p.A.

Contents

We need energy

You use energy for everything you do. Just
reading this book uses some of your energy.
You get this energy from the food you eat.
Energy is also used to heat and light our homes,
shops and factories.

*Petrol is a fuel used in cars. Smoke from petrol gives off gases
which pollute the air we breathe.*

If we carry on using all the Earth's fossil fuels so quickly, rigs will soon have no more oil to drill up.

Most of the world's energy is still made by burning coal, oil and gas. These are known as fossil fuels. The world today uses more and more energy. One day the fossil fuels will all be used up.

Scientists are looking at new and safer ways to make the power we need. One of the ways is power from the Earth. This is the natural heat that is found under the ground.

Heat under our feet

Energy from the wind, waves and the Sun will never run out. It is clean and it lasts forever. Energy from the Earth will run out, but there is lots of it. If we are careful, we can use the underground heat to give us energy without harming the planet.

This is what the inside of Earth looks like.

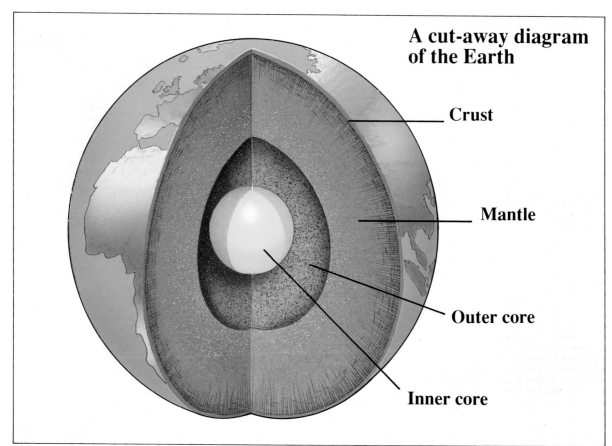

A cut-away diagram of the Earth

Crust

Mantle

Outer core

Inner core

The inner core of the Earth is made of boiling hot metals. The mantle is hot, but solid rock. The crust is the part of the Earth that we live on.

In some places the crust is very thin. The hot rock, or lava, breaks through, like in the diagram on the right. Places such as these have volcanoes.

It is difficult to use the energy from volcanoes. They are too hot and powerful.

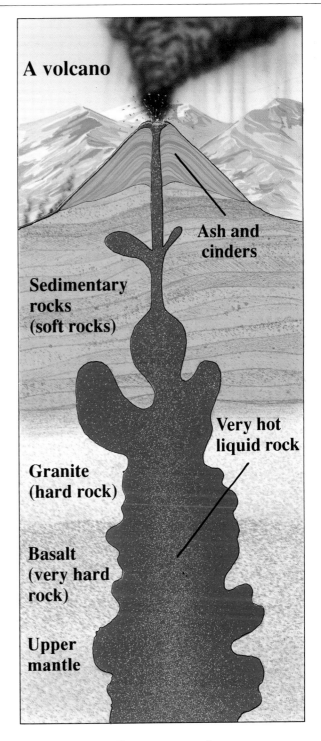

How a volcano works.

This geyser is in Yellowstone Park in the USA.

In some areas where volcanoes occur, water collects underground in between the hot rocks.

The water becomes hot and turns into steam.
It pushes its way through the Earth's surface
and shoots high into the air, making geysers.

The diagram below shows one way of using hot spring water to heat our homes, farms or leisure centres.

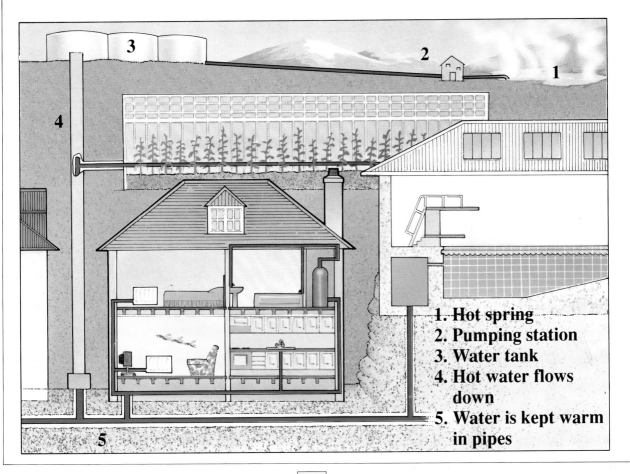

1. Hot spring
2. Pumping station
3. Water tank
4. Hot water flows down
5. Water is kept warm in pipes

Making steam

1. The atoms are not very warm yet, so they are not moving.

2. As the atoms get warmer, they move around. Some escape as steam.

3. When the water is boiling, more and more atoms escape as steam.

What happens when water is heated?

Water is made up of millions of atoms. These atoms are too small to be seen. As water becomes hot, the atoms move.

When the water reaches 100°C it turns to steam. Now the atoms move very quickly, taking up a lot of space. This makes the pressure inside the kettle grow and the steam escapes through the spout.

In the same way, the pressure from the underground hot water builds up. The steam pushes its way out of the ground as a geyser.

Hot spring water can be fun as well as useful. People can swim in this water, used to make power at a power station in Iceland.

In the past

Animals and people have always liked to live near warm places. The ancient Greek and Japanese people liked to bathe in hot springs. They believed the water would keep them healthy.

These Japanese monkeys live near pools of hot water to keep themselves warm during the cold winters.

The Romans built a spa in Bath in England.

Spa-water contains minerals or salts, which
are good for health.

These Japanese people have found a clever way to use warm sand! Lying in it helps them to feel relaxed and well.

For hundreds of years, the Maori people in New Zealand have used heat from rocks and water to cook their food.

In Iceland the hot springs were also used for washing and cooking.

Power from the Earth usually has to be used near to where it is found. This is because the water gets cold as it goes along the pipes carrying it to cities.

A solution is to use the steam. The steam turns a machine called a generator which makes electricity. The electricity is later used at the time and the place where it is needed.

This is the world's first power station using energy from the Earth. It is in Italy, in a town called Larderello.

More than just hot water

This diagram shows how rainwater collects under the ground. It trickles into cracks in the rocks. The place where the water collects is called an aquifer.

Underneath the aquifer is a layer of hot, hard rocks. The rocks keep the water in place and heat it up.

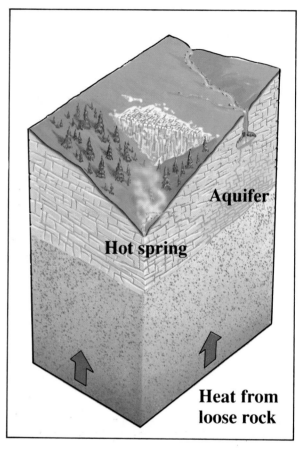

Aquifer

Hot spring

Heat from loose rock

Look at all the colours of the rocks around this geyser.

The water in the middle of hot springs is very hot. It is always ready to bubble up and over the rocks.

Chemicals from the spring water in geysers wash over the rocks and become hard, making strange shapes and colours.

Opposite bottom *A hot spring.*

When the water is used for heating, the chemicals can damage the water pipes. To stop this happening, the heat is passed to a fresh supply of water and this is used instead.

This town is in Iceland. Hot water pipes run under the streets and through people's houses. Office blocks, swimming pools and homes are all heated by the hot water!

This greenhouse is kept warm all through the year by power from the Earth.

Power from the Earth costs half as much as any other type of energy that Iceland could use.

Power stations that use energy from the Earth can be found in Italy, New Zealand and Japan. The biggest power stations are in California in an area called Little Geysers.

This power station uses power from hot water. It is in Hawaii.

More of the amazing shapes made from the hardened chemicals in spring water can be seen in this photograph of Pamukkale in Turkey.

Areas of natural springs are not always nice to look at or to be near. Sometimes they are even dangerous.

Spring water can contain dangerous chemicals.

Heat from rocks

The map below shows the area known as the Ring of Fire where most volcanoes are found.

Often, even though the rocks around these places are extremely hot, there is no underground water. Scientists have had to think of a way to use the heat.

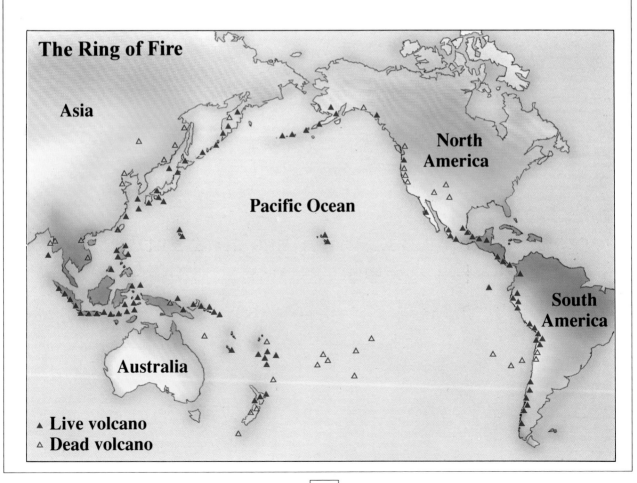

The Ring of Fire

Asia

North America

Pacific Ocean

South America

Australia

▲ Live volcano
△ Dead volcano

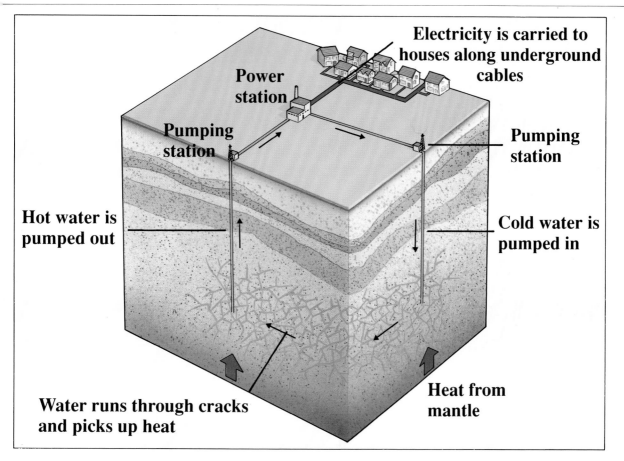

The above diagram shows a way of using heat from rocks.

Water is pumped down a pipe from one pumping station. The water fills up the little cracks in the hot underground rocks. It becomes hot. It is then pumped up another pipe by a second pumping station.

The hot water is made into steam and sent on to a power station. Here, it is used to make electricity.

The drilling rigs for a Hot Dry Rocks power station in Cornwall, England. The project began in 1976 and it cost over £33 million.

This Hot Dry Rocks power station pumps cold water into hot rocks and then pumps hot water back up again.

Power from the Earth causes less pollution than using fossil fuels. But the actual power stations can be quite ugly. Also, the gas which is sometimes found in the water makes a horrible smell – very much like rotten eggs!

Wairakei power station

Wairakei is in New Zealand. It has many geysers and hot springs.

In 1950, engineers started looking for hot water under the ground. They wanted the hot water to make electricity in a power station.

The power station at Wairakei.

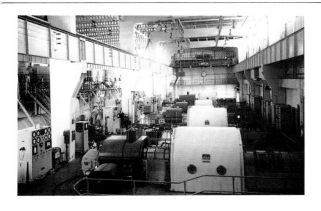

This huge room gets the water to make electricity from over 60 wells!

Scientists have discovered that Wairakei has much more underground hot water than they thought at first.

The government of New Zealand now hopes that the heat will not be used up for many, many more years.

It is exciting to think that the Earth has such a big store of heat just waiting to be used to give us clean and cheap energy.

People are still drilling for hot water in Wairakei.

Make a hot spring

Make this hot spring to see if you can trap energy from hot water. You must ask a grown-up to help you.

You need

an old metal cocoa tin, 2 lollipop sticks, string, a saucer, an egg cup, plasticine, a candle, tin foil, a piece of coat hanger wire and 2 bricks.

1. Ask a grown-up to make a hole in the lid of the cocoa tin.

2. Tie the lollipop sticks tightly to each side of the tin with the string. Then pour a little water into the tin. Put the lid back on.

3. Put the saucer on to the tin foil and draw around it. Cut out the shape – it should be a circle. Draw another circle shape inside using an egg cup.

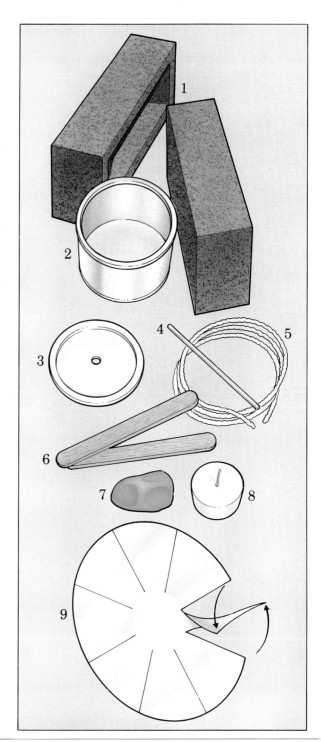

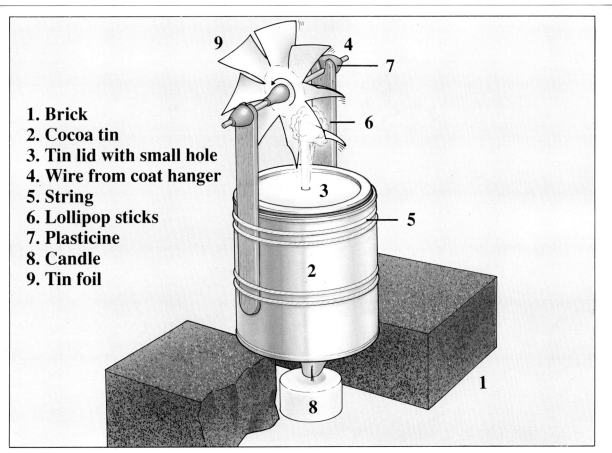

1. Brick
2. Cocoa tin
3. Tin lid with small hole
4. Wire from coat hanger
5. String
6. Lollipop sticks
7. Plasticine
8. Candle
9. Tin foil

4. Look at the diagram on page 28. Can you see how the big circle has been divided into eight parts. Cut each part towards the middle circle. Then fold each part outwards a little to make a windmill.

5. Push the piece of coat hanger wire through the middle of the windmill.

6. Fix the coat hanger wire to the lollipop sticks with plasticine. Make sure the windmill is above the hole in the cocoa tin lid.

7. Ask a grown-up to light the candle. Put the candle under the tin, between the two bricks.

Soon steam should start to come out of the hole in the top of the tin and turn the windmill. TAKE CARE! Steam is very hot. Do not put your hands near the steam. Also, do not touch the candle when it is alight, or for half an hour after it has gone out.

Glossary

Acid rain Rainwater made acid by smoke from power stations and factories.

Ammonia A type of gas.

Atmosphere The layer of gases that surrounds the Earth.

Atoms All things are made up of millions of atoms. The atoms themselves are too small to be seen.

Fossil fuels Fuels like coal, oil or gas. They are the remains of plants and animals that lived millions of years ago.

Geysers Springs under the ground which shoot out hot water and steam.

Hot springs Pools of very hot water that are found in certain countries, such as Iceland.

Minerals Types of rocks which are found in the Earth. Our bodies need tiny amounts of some minerals in order to stay healthy.

Volcanoes Mountains which can explode and throw out hot ashes and burning rocks.

Books to read

Electricity by Graham Peacock (Wayland, 1992)

Energy by Deborah Elliott (Wayland, 1993)

My Science Book of Electricity by Neil Ardley (Dorling Kindersley, 1991)

My Science Book of Energy by Neil Ardley (Dorling Kindersley, 1992)

Index